EXTREME NATURE

FEARSOME FORCES OF NATURE

Anita Ganeri

Raintree
Chicago, Illinois

www.capstonepub.com
Visit our website to find out
more information about
Heinemann-Raintree books.

To order:
☎ Phone 800-747-4992
💻 Visit www.capstonepub.com
to browse our catalog and order online.

© 2013 Raintree
an imprint of Capstone Global Library, LLC
Chicago, Illinois

Edited by Dan Nunn, Rebecca Rissman,
 and Catherine Veitch
Designed by Cynthia Della-Rovere
Picture research by Tracy Cummins
Production by Alison Parsons

Originated by Capstone Global Library
Printed and bound in China by CTPS

18 17 16
10 9 8 7 6 5 4

**Library of Congress Cataloging-in-Publication
Data**
Ganeri, Anita
Fearsome forces of nature / Anita Ganeri.—1st ed.
p. cm.—(Extreme nature)
Includes bibliographical references and index.
ISBN 978-1-4109-4696-6 (hb)—ISBN 978-1-4109-
4701-7 (pb) 1. Science—Miscellanea—Juvenile
literature. 2. Nature—Miscellanea—Juvenile literature.
I. Title.
Q173.G336 2013
500—dc23   2011038390

Acknowledgments
We would like to thank the following for permission to
reproduce photographs: AP Photo p. 9 (Pat Roque);
Corbis pp. 5 (© KYODO/REUTERS), 12 (© Jim Wark/
Visuals Unlimited), 14 (© ROB GRIFFIT/epa), 16
(© Xinhua/Xinhua Press), 17 (© Kyodo/XinHua/
Xinhua Press), 19 (© STR/epa), 23 (© Chris Hellier),
26 (© JEAN-CHRISTOPHE BOTT/epa); Getty Images
pp. 4 (Art Wolfe), 6 (Peter Carsten), 8 (James P. Blair),
13 (The Asahi Shimbun), 15 (YOSHIKAZU TSUNO/
AFP), 18 (HIROSHI KAWAHARA/AFP), 25 (JOSE
NAVARRO/AFP); Shutterstock pp. 22 (© Yory
Frenklakh), 7 (© beboy),10 (© PavelSvoboda), 11
(© Lee Prince), 20 (© akva), 21 (© rm), 24 (© Kapu),
27 (© deepspacedave).

Cover photograph of a volcanic eruption reproduced
with permission of Shutterstock (© beboy).
Background photograph of fire reproduced with
permission of Shutterstock (© Mettus).

Every effort has been made to contact copyright
holders of material reproduced in this book. Any
omissions will be rectified in subsequent printings if
notice is given to the publisher.

Disclaimer
All the Internet addresses (URLs) given in this book
were valid at the time of going to press. However, due
to the dynamic nature of the Internet, some addresses
may have changed, or sites may have changed or
ceased to exist since publication. While the author and
publisher regret any inconvenience this may cause
readers, no responsibility for any such changes can be
accepted by either the author or the publisher.

Some words are shown in bold, **like this**. You can find
out what they mean by looking in the glossary.

Contents

What Are Forces of Nature?

Did you know that Earth has about 1,500 **active volcanoes**? Fearsome forces of nature happen all over the world. You can read more about them in this book. You can also find out what people do when nature turns nasty.

DID YOU KNOW?
Earthquakes can tear roads apart and bring down bridges.

Violent Volcanoes

A **volcano** is a place where red-hot, liquid rock bursts through the surface of Earth. Below ground, the rock is called **magma**. When it reaches the surface, it is called **lava**. When a volcano **erupts**, hot gas, ash, and dust are blasted into the air.

lava

DID YOU KNOW?
Lava can reach a temperature of a scorching 2,200°F! That is 12 times hotter than boiling water!

Mount Saint Helens

Some **volcanoes erupt** quite gently. Others explode with a bang. In 1980, Mount Saint Helens, in Washington state, erupted. The blast was so powerful that it blew half of the mountain away.

People living near volcanoes sometimes have to be **evacuated** from their homes.

Gushing Geysers

A **geyser** is a hole in the ground that spurts out steam and hot water. Red-hot rocks under ground heat up the water. Then the geyser blows.

The water and steam can shoot more than 164 feet into the air. That is five times as high as a house!

DID YOU KNOW?
Old Faithful geyser, in Wyoming, blows roughly every 90 minutes.

Shaking Earth

The surface of Earth is called its **crust**. Earth's hard crust is cracked into pieces. Sometimes the pieces push and slide past each other. If this happens suddenly, an earthquake can shake the ground.

The San Andreas Fault, in California, lies along a crack in Earth's crust.

Earthquakes can break up roads and make buildings fall down.

DID YOU KNOW?

Most earthquakes last for less than one minute.

Rescue teams work hard to save many people who have been buried under the rubble from fallen buildings.

rubble

In February 2011, a huge earthquake struck Christchurch, in New Zealand. The city was badly damaged, and 181 people were killed.

DID YOU KNOW?
In school, Japanese children practice regular earthquake **drills**.

Terrifying Tsunamis

Earthquakes under the sea cause **tsunamis**. The sudden shock moves a huge amount of water, which races across the sea in waves.

DID YOU KNOW?
At sea, a tsunami travels as fast as a jet plane.

The tsunami waves get higher as they reach land.

17

When a **tsunami** reaches land, the waves crash onto the shore. They can flood towns, rip up trees, and sweep buildings, cars, and people away.

During the 2011 tsunami in Japan, the ground shook for around 3 to 5 minutes. Thousands of people died, and millions lost their homes.

Raging Rivers

Flowing water is hugely powerful. It can slowly carve through solid rock to make **canyons** and caves. It can also crash over the side of a mountain, plunging down as a waterfall.

Grand Canyon, Arizona

DID YOU KNOW?
Angel Falls in Venezuela is the world's highest waterfall. It is taller than two Empire State Buildings!

Crashing Coasts

Along **coasts**, waves smash hard into cliffs. The waves carry rocks and stones that wear cliffs away and carve out holes and other features.

These houses are in danger of falling into the sea.

Awful Avalanches

An **avalanche** is a massive pile of snow that suddenly breaks loose and crashes down a mountain. An avalanche can speed downhill as fast as a race car.

An avalanche can bury walkers, skiers, and even whole villages. Some mountain villages have special steel fences around them, to slow down any falling snow.

Avalanches can strike without any warning. People can be buried in the snow. Helicopters search for survivors from the air. On the ground, rescuers use long sticks, called snow probes, to feel for people in the snow.

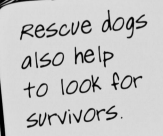

Rescue dogs also help to look for survivors.

Quiz: What Am I?

Read the clues, then try to figure out "What am I?" Find the answers at the bottom of page 29. But guess first!

1) I come out of a **volcano**.
I can be as hot as 2,200°F.
I start off as **magma**.
What am I?

2) I'm made of steam and hot water.
I spurt out of the ground.
I can be more than 164 feet high.
What am I?

3) I usually last for less than one minute.
I make the ground shake.
I can shake buildings down.
What am I?

4) I start off at sea.
I get higher as I reach land.
I can travel as fast as a jet plane.
What am I?

5) I can bury a whole village.
I can move as fast as a race car.
I happen in the mountains.
What am I?

Glossary

active able to erupt at any time

avalanche massive pile of snow that crashes down a mountain

canyon deep gash in the ground, carved out by water

coast edge of the land that borders the sea

crust hard, rocky outside of Earth

drill practice for what to do in the event of something like a fire or earthquake

erupt burst or explode with lava

evacuate move out of the way of danger

geyser jet of hot water and steam that shoots out of the ground

lava magma that has come to Earth's surface

magma runny, red-hot rock under ground

tsunami series of waves set off by an undersea earthquake or volcano

volcano hole in the ground where red-hot rock comes out

Find Out More

Books

Ganeri, Anita. *Eruption!: The Story of Volcanoes.* New York: Dorling Kindersley, 2010.

Shone, Rob, and Gary Jeffrey. *Graphic Natural Disasters* series. New York: Rosen, 2007.

Spilsbury, Louise, and Richard Spilsbury. *Awesome Forces of Nature* series. Chicago: Heinemann Library, 2011.

Websites

www.nationalgeographic.com/ forcesofnature/film/kids.html

This National Geographic Website is packed with games, activities, and true stories about forces of nature.

kids.nationalgeographic.com/kids/stories/ spacescience/freaky-forces-of-nature

Another National Geographic Website, this one focuses on 10 freaky forces of nature.

Index